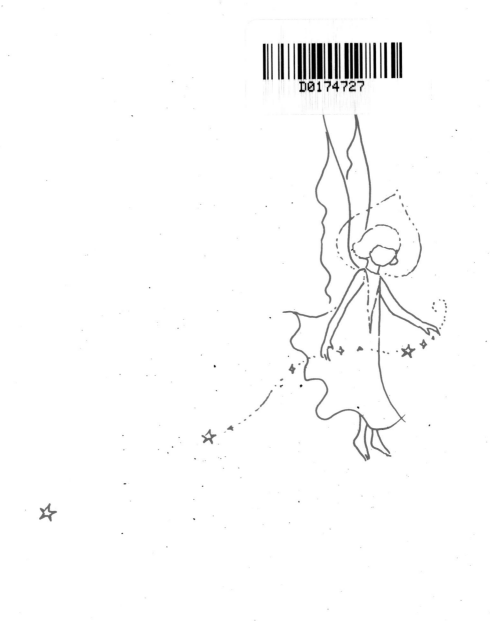

To: _____

From: _____

ANGEL PRAYERS

by **SAMARA ANJELAE**
illustrated by **ANCA HARITON**

BelleTress Books

BelleTress Books

BelleTress Books, P.O. Box 922, Paris, KY. 40361.
©2003 by Samara Anjelae. All Rights Reserved.
Illustrations ©2003 by Anca Hariton. All Rights Reserved.
©1994 by Sally O. Sharp.

Published 1994. Second Edition 2003
Printed in China
07 06 05 04   5 4 3 2
Library of Congress Catalog Card Number 94-60856
ISBN: 0-9708754-6-0

www.belletressbooks.com

Dedication

We never walk alone, even when we think we do. This book is dedicated to our loved ones who have walked on earth and now who are in spirit sharing their love and wisdom. May we take a few moments to recognize our seen and unseen helpers. We say an Angel Prayer for you.

Table of Contents

Introduction

Angel Prayers came to me effortlessly and lovingly.
I can only explain it as if an angel delivered the words to me,
knowing that if I had to repeat the writing I probably could not. It
is said we always teach what we need to learn the most. I was given
these words for my learning and growth.

In this second edition Anca Hariton interprets each angel prayer, her
exquisite illustrations bring you even closer to the angel you need for that
moment, day, week or lifetime.

Whether read silently or aloud – to yourself or to your children and family –
I hope Angel Prayers bring comfort, direction and wisdom to you as they have
to me.

Blessings and Love to all,

Samara Anjelae

Angel of
Attraction

If you have love and goodness in your heart, you reflect love and goodness. If you have respect and humility for yourself, you reflect respect and humility. Each thought you have carries an energy that is sent out to the universe.

Keep your thoughts positive and guided with love, honesty and goodwill towards all of humankind.

☆

Bring what you want in your life first to your thoughts, and watch your ideas manifest themselves. Your actions reflect your beliefs.

Let all thoughts vibrate with love. You can have true happiness and serenity when you let go of the idea that material possessions can bring happiness. Know that happiness comes from within. By creating good for others, you create good for yourself.

Like attracts like. The positive energy you reflect attracts the positive energy of others. When all thoughts are centered on God, then you have found your one true attraction.

☆

Angel of
Belonging

*F*eeling and being alone goes against our nature to be at one with God. When it is happening it is very real, confusing and sad. Many souls try to escape from the feeling of isolation. To feel you do not belong under any circumstance is very overwhelming, but we are really never alone. We have to look inside and muster up enough love and courage to know that we deserve to be one with our Creator. The way we treat our fellowkind aids in our feeling of belonging. Going against one another serves no purpose. When actions and good deeds are done to aid others, we are then working for the higher good of all. As we move rapidly in our lives, we forget these principles. This adds to the lonely feeling.

Do not make people feel more alone than they already are. Touch others to assure them that you care. The more you give to others, the more you will receive. Feel the presence of God. Call upon the energy of the universe and you will be supplied with the strength and love to carry you through. Trust and companionship will replace the emptiness.

Angel of
Blessings

Blessings are bestowed on all, but many do not know of these gifts. Blessings can come in many sacred forms. Because they are so different, often they do not look like blessings. The wise soul will know its blessings. Those who are trapped by their own limitations and thoughts do not see the beauty and the truth of these wondrous gifts. We often look at others and feel they are more blessed than we. When we start looking at our blessings without comparing them to others, we discover more support and grace. Let the truth be known. We are all blessed with an abundance of gifts, but with different gifts.

Blessings begin with every breath and step we take. Give thanks and honor all the Divine gifts that come to you. Create a new vision by seeing from a different angle with a fresh perspective. Trust in the power of goodness, the power of God.

Work with what you have and pray for the blessing you need to be given to you. Follow your sacred path and make a difference in your own life. This will draw love and peace to you. You will then make a difference in the lives of others. Walk, breathe and be truly blessed.

Angel of Change

To cleanse your thoughts and make changes, you must be willing to look at what is under the surface. To reveal yourself and accept your true form can be initially painful. It is through pain and honesty that you reach an important stage. It is a place where self-acceptance is embraced. A new path will open with the cleansing of old patterns and harmful beliefs. Wisdom will be gained.

Change is inevitable. Many resist change for fear of the uncertain. Change makes the process of life unfold. By accepting new opportunities, we leave behind that which is not working. Sometimes we are forced to change without any control over the situation. It could be through a painful event or an emotional experience. Our eyes of wisdom may be temporarily blinded because of the pain. However, it is through these times the soul completes a learning phase, grows in knowledge and attains wisdom. Sometimes, it is hard to understand this growth on a physical level, but your soul knows what is needed for development. The same is true when wonderful events happen. The soul can move to higher vibrations in joyful as well as in grieving times. It all depends on how your thoughts and actions are used throughout the course.

There is a lesson in every situation. You have the choice to decide whether or not you want to grow from it. May all who are experiencing change bring their faith to the surface. God provides all that is needed. Believe, trust and see.

Angel of Choice

*F*or some it is difficult to look in the mirror and see themselves. *Until acceptance comes from within, the soul remains stagnant in development. When love and understanding are attained by the soul, a deeper understanding occurs. The world seems different. The mind opens up to new avenues. Progress is made when the mind leaves one stage and ascends gracefully to the next. Spiritual guidance is available for those wanting and waiting to take the journey. Guidance that is soft and loving, not harsh or dogmatic, can lead you to your answers.*

Beliefs and opinions can be so strong that we put up a wall to shield us from any truth or wisdom which we do not understand. Each being has the choice in what direction to take. Sometimes we learn by taking the challenging direction. The important part is that we learn by doing.

The way to recognize the higher path is by listening to the voice inside, the voice that speaks when respect is given. If we do not treat our own thoughts as valid information, we discredit ourselves. The beauty of life is having the choice to change what is not working and try something that does work. There are many ways to take you where you are going, some are just more graceful than others. Walk openly to new beginnings.

☆

Angel of Clarity

*T*his, too, shall pass. Change is constant. Know that you do not have to stay in one place. When you suffer from frustration, try to look at the root of the problem. Step outside the situation and see the cause. Be patient and kind to yourself. Do not try to force a solution. Answers will eventually come. Let the frustration pass and clear the mind before making decisions. Many times we haven't received all the information that is needed to make a decision. Ask that God provide the resources to move you out of the challenging moment. Take what you learn from every experience and use it wisely in the next situation.

Life experiences are our way to grow. Move forward, not backward. Learn from your mistakes and continue having successes. We have advances and setbacks to teach and prepare us. Tomorrow is a new day. Greet it with gratitude from what you have learned today.

Angel of Commitment

Commitment to an idea, purpose, person or thing brings results. To achieve inner joy we must commit ourselves to do what is needed to meet our goals. With the help, love and support from the universe, we can make progress. Effort and strength lead the way to growth and rewards. In times of confusion and hardship, we can choose to let go of the struggles and listen to the guidance of our inner voice. As we let go of our fear and ego, we learn to commit to our true goals. The soul that works with and not against itself is the soul that will rise above the challenges. The truth and wisdom of our inner voice will tell us which goals are worthy and which are unrealistic adventures.

Facing the true self takes an honest and open approach. Laying blame on others for our lack of commitment only prolongs the advancement of obtaining our goals. We create our own happiness or unhappiness. The beauty of life is that we control our own growth. Take time to look and see what new seeds of ideas have been planted within you. Let them grow and blossom. As the truth of new ideas comes forth, review your commitments to your goals. Be willing to abandon old goals for better ones as your knowledge and wisdom grow. Flexibility is as important a part of commitment, as is steadfastness.

Angel of
Compassion

To look at the past will help explain the direction of the future. Your soul receives certain understanding and growth throughout its evolution. Once the knowledge is learned it becomes important how it is used. Some refuse to learn from past mistakes and actions. Fear is usually the answer. With more insight into the everlasting life fear disappears, and more people feel safe on their journeys. Positive loving words must be spoken. Compassionate energy needs to be released and shared.

Compassion will provide a start for those who are suffering and in pain. Unfortunately, minds sometimes comprehend only what is apparent therefore cannot understand why things happen as they do. Many are afraid to ask for help or direction, but it is there if only they would ask.

For the lonely who feel abandoned by their families, loved ones, friends, or society, do not give up hope. You are loved. You have friends seen and unseen. They will love you, care for you and protect you. Your thoughts are heard. Your energy is felt. God does not abandon. God is the source of all love. Believe. Love, peace and serenity are achievable and attainable to everyone, no matter where you are in your life.

Angel of Creativity

Create what you want by believing in yourself and in the universe to provide what you need. Let go of past fears or blocks you are holding onto. Today is a new day to reach within and bring out the good. Take charge and change what is not working in your life. With progress you will find yourself surrounded by thoughts of peace and harmony, and soon you will be enveloped in a peaceful and harmonious environment.

Creating is the finest form of expression. Be an expression of God. Let your energy manifest into a creation that you can call your own. Expression comes in many ways, some seen and some unseen. In times of discontent and in times of tranquillity you can be productive by releasing thoughts into tangible items. When the mind works with the soul, then the body creates.

Blocks of suppressed energy are freed when the soul is allowed to express. When the expression is mixed with love, then a creation of beauty exists. Children often possess the true sense of creativity. Their world is full of unconditional expression. When we incorporate passion and creativity into our work and lives, we allow our inner selves to express outwardly. Our creativity is always changing and expanding as the soul expands and grows to added heights. When love accompanies the journey of expression, creativity is at its best. Go and create.

☆

Angel of
Desires

Your heart knows good from evil.
Place your desires in the energy of light.
Release any desires that are not for your
highest good or for the highest good of others.
Search within to find your desires that serve you
and humankind. Bring the beauty of balance into
your every thought. As you fill your soul with Divine
wisdom and knowledge, your every desire of spiritual
love will hold true. Take the steps to find that inner
truth of knowing.

The desires of today will be the reality of tomorrow. Be free from limitations and embrace the ideas that help you create your desires. Walk with confidence and speak with love. Let God guide you to the path where your desires flow naturally. Trust in your journey as you take the steps to bring passion, talent and rewards into your life.

Angel of
Faith

*F*aith is the belief in the power
of God. Faith dispels fear. Go within
and reach for faith. Your every need
is provided. Shift to a new awareness.
Discover the power within to lead
you to safety. Turn to the light for
answers. Let the light shine in the
dark corners of fear. Take time to
quiet the mind and allow the
answers to come. To have faith is to
have God in your heart, peace in
your soul, and strength in your
body. As you practice having

faith, inspirations turn into ideas that bring solutions and gifts. Trust in your inner self. Your soul knows faith. Find faith and you will live the truth as a child of God, at one with God.

Fear is a lack of belief in the power of God. Fear has no power against faith. Take time to calm the mind. You create you own fear by listening to outer circumstances. Turn to the Creator for the comfort and security you need. Bring love to your body and mind by concentrating on your oneness with God. Step outside the situation and release it. Carrying around fear, anger, and resentment brings stress and sickness, emotional and physical. Let harmony flow through your body as you attract the light of hope and peace. God gives hope and you create the peace. With peace in your heart, your soul is at home. Make a home built around God and there you will find the love and faith you so desire and need.

Angel of
Forgiveness

The ability to forgive is a true test of growth. When the heart and mind are in conflict, the body carries the stress of the situation. Carrying anger and resentment is not in the body's best interest. The body gets sick. If resentment is carried for long periods of time, the body becomes a home for disease.

How do you learn to forgive, especially if much harm and hurt have taken place? Trust the universe to provide the proper action. The wise soul knows that we reap what we sow. When we learn to forgive others, we also learn to forgive ourselves. True forgiving comes from the heart. Words cannot create the feeling. Serenity replaces resentment and anger. The process of letting go differs for each soul. Some souls must experience different phases of hurt and anger for their own growth.

Let go of what you cannot control and accept your responsibilities. Peace and a shift in consciousness will come. This lays a smoother foundation for the next lesson on forgiveness. The soul who forgives and releases their resentment, moves to a place of tranquillity and serenity. Forgiveness is the key to your own liberation.

If you truly forgive, then it reflects in your life and provides encouragement and hope for those around you. During this time when you need to be forgiven or need to forgive someone, reach out and ask for angelic help.

Angel of
Friendship

The love of a true friend is unconditional. The corollary is also true. You are not someone's true friend unless you love them unconditionally. True friends supports us and gives us strength during our most difficult times. True friends are priceless gifts. But choose your friends with care. Check with your heart to see if the love and concern they show for you is real, or if they have other motives for being your friend.

Be a supportive friend and set your standards high. Your friends are reflections of you. When you share the company of others and there is good, then good will come from them. When you share the company of those that bring harm to others, then you are harming yourself.

*Trust your heart to know if a person
is a true friend, and also if you are a true
friend to another. Open your mind to let
love and friendship come into your life
and you will have it. You deserve to be
with others who share in your goodness.
When you practice unconditional love
and forgiveness, you will attract
others who express the same.
Be a true friend and
find a true friend.*

Angel of Gifts

The heart is at peace when the gifts given at birth are fully used. Every soul has many talents and unique skills that can be tapped into and developed. Experience the joy when you use these gifts to create an expression of you. Do not let fear get in the way. Have faith, work sincerely and rewards will come. Be open to the Divine wisdom that is yours. Bring forth your passion and your love and let the energy of creativity manifest into a creation of your own. Handle your ideas with patience, hope and trust.

Know when the time is right success will become apparent. With persistence and a positive attitude, greatness comes. Trust your intuitive thoughts and go with them.

You are most in harmony when you follow your heart. Know that you have the power within you to bring dreams to reality through your rare gifts. You are a creative spirit. You can bring solutions to your problems. Go beyond the limits. Visualize your hopes and goals. Surround yourself with the light of love, the light of direction. When you receive an idea and it feels right in your heart, then follow it. Ideas are of little value until they are put to use.

Angel of Giving

To appreciate the energy that brings fulfillment to our lives is to appreciate every waking breath. With every breath and every step, we have the power to rise and develop our wisdom within, the wisdom that leads to a connection to all life and matter.

Witnessing a union of energy reveals the great mysteries of life. Witnessing the union of thoughts reveals the likeness we share and the unlimited potential we have. Looking within and reaching within connects our soul to the Infinite Spirit who created us.

Raising the degree of vibration and consciousness brings a release of rewards to all who share in the radiant energy. Praying and putting a loving touch on the many hearts that need healing reaps a stream of positive flow. To give a gift is to receive a wave of God's desire. A loving gift that is unconditionally given to another will be returned to you tenfold. Take time and look at all the loving gifts that can be given and go spread the love. Not only will it spread and grow, but also the true meaning of our existence will be answered.

Angel of Gratitude

Today is time for thanks. Every
day is a time for thanks. When we can
appreciate the simplest of gifts even in
times of confusion and hardships,
then we move forward.

A soul that appreciates the gifts of living, the true gifts, will reap rewards from being grateful and appreciative. Prayers are heard and answered. Prayers of thanks are highly important. They work with the soul for the highest good. As with anything, simply acknowledging the opportunity to experience the moment is of value. Be aware and respectful of all gifts offered to us. The wise soul can look at all situations as a way for personal growth and advancement.

Those who suffer must know that the grief will pass and be replaced with invaluable insight and softer emotions.

Go all the way and you will find what you need. You will find what is always there: an infinite supply of love and energy. For God forsakes no one. Give thanks for today, give thanks for you. For without you, there would not be this moment now. As you know, there will always be you. Your soul will remain forever. Treat your soul right, and start by thanking God for your unique being, beauty and potential.

Angel of Growth

T here is a time for learning and growing. If you walk the path with God in your heart, truth and beauty will unfold before you. Trust and the way will be shown. Keep the mind and body clear and your mission will prevail. The art of giving and seeking will bring results. Rest, relax and then move. Move in the direction where serenity can come and the heart can be at peace. This comes from doing the work that brings you physical and spiritual satisfaction. Steps that you take to seek wisdom will provide the foundation.

Clear the inner self from all fears and worries. Ask that you be shown the way.

Messengers are here to assist. Information and direction will come. With each step taken, the love of God surrounds you.

Learning and growing will come naturally. When you cease to expand your learning, you are not using your potential. The mind then becomes idle and more difficult to change. To grow means to open and feel the energy of living. One trace of revived energy can be a beginning for added creations.

Inspiration comes from many directions. Deep inside of us there is a wealth of information and valuable ideas. The key is to tap into this potential. Why let it go to waste? Let your ideas bring helpful and loving assistance to you and others. The more we help others, the more help is given back to us. When we go against this principle we are in conflict with our soul. Today grow into the great soul that you are.

Angel of Guidance

*R*esults happen when the belief in everlasting life is truly accepted. Everyday challenges can be met with more understanding and ease. The struggles may still be difficult, but understanding takes place on a soul level. The lessons to be learned are goals to be achieved. Your soul was put here to work out the lessons and live a rich and fulfilling life.

The walk through life needs to bring in higher vibrations to continually ease the conflicts. You will be guided to new avenues and to new solutions. All souls can guide other souls by providing assistance and direction.

More and more people will be looking for spiritual guidance, guidance that is soft and embracing, guidance that will enable all to be accepted on their own paths. The foundation of this guidance comes from the universal spark that is common to all souls. Healing is essential. We carry emotional scars and blockages from our past. The more we release the past, the better the physical body functions, and the quicker our soul reaches greater understanding.

Angel of Happiness

Happiness is the result of blending love with faith. God is love. When we live our lives with the belief that all are equal in the eyes of God, we can love others as we love ourselves. Love starts within and grows outward. To see beauty in all and to walk the path of wisdom brings the soul to true awakening. As we share the moments of harmony, energy surrounds us with complete serenity. To respect all creation is love. May we find more love in our hearts.

Happiness is finding yourself and knowing the truth, the truth that you always be a part of the Divine plan. There is no reason to live in fear and distress. Walk with God in your heart and you will be protected. Happiness will fill every cell in your body. Even in turbulent times a soul can have true happiness. There is a place of serenity. It resides in your soul. It is knowing that Divine order is taking place. It is having a trust in our Creator. Find your happiness by living your spiritual path today.

Angel of Harmony

B lessed are we that share in the abundance of love that God provides. If people could see beyond their own troubles and look further, they would see a place exists in harmony. Souls need each other to give and receive love.

How do you measure your attempt to reach for that space where only loving and peaceful thoughts reside? The measure is up to the soul to decide. Inside of us there is a depth of understanding waiting to be explored. You will not need to ask if you have reached it *when you are there. You will know. It is an opportunity that every soul, young and old, has the ability to reach.*

You must have harmony within before you can project it to others. You must know your soul and pursue the path of unity with God by living, actually living, life. Even the most troubled souls long to know the answers to life. They long to know they are truly loved. They long to know that there is a better way. Everyone can have a beautiful journey.

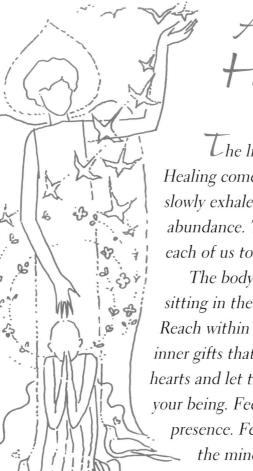

Angel of Healing

*T*he light of healing surrounds us. Healing comes as one breathes in and slowly exhales the Divine energy of abundance. The riches of life are stored in each of us to enjoy.

The body and soul can be healed by sitting in the silence of one's thoughts. Reach within and bring to the surface the inner gifts that are available. Open your hearts and let the energy charge every fiber of your being. Feel the beauty of angelic presence. Feel the beauty of God. Clear the mind long enough to appreciate *the wisdom of the soul. We all need to give and receive more love. There is never too much love. And there is never too much healing.*

All needs are met in abundance if we walk the path where the spirit of good exists. Healing begins with you. Listen to what you say. Do you speak with love and kindness? Watch how you treat yourself. Do you act with love and kindness? With discipline, we learn to nourish our bodies and minds with healthy food and healthy thoughts. When you are ready to begin the healing, center all thoughts toward love and balance. God is love. Know as you heal, emotions are released from the body. If there is anger, resentment, guilt or shame to be released let it go. To be centered, continually turn your thoughts back to love. Angels are channels of love and light. Let their light come to you and bring rays of healing love.

Angel of
Health

*In times of sickness, a cleansing takes place.
Let the body rid itself of the toxic poisons and
make room for health and harmony in every cell.
Call upon the angels to help you in your healing.*

Angels bring light rays of miracles. Ask for their help and believe in their healing touch, invisible to some, but known in heart by all. Embrace the energy with the desire to be healed, and as your soul heals the emotional body, the physical body responds.

Never give up hope. Even if you need medical attention know the power of your thoughts mixed with the power of God makes the healing possible. Be still and be open to your own angels. They may appear as radiant balls of light or as inspirations of a peaceful idea. Or you may simply feel their presence. Wherever you go and wherever you are, angels of love and healing are surrounding you. Ask with sincerity and watch harmony surround you in thought and body.

Angel of
Hope

Join hands across the world. Join hearts across the world. Put aside differences. Appreciate that we are all beings of love wanting love and needing love. Look at each other with love and hope, not with hate and despair. Do not judge, just accept. Wrap positive thoughts around each other for comfort and warmth. Come out of the cold and dark to the sunlight of hope. Grow with vibrations of peace and spread them to everyone.

Strength comes when wisdom is gained. Every path leads to a solution. It is an aspiration to help all to the path where inner peace resides.

Love is a powerful word that needs to be heard and felt by many. Many have been on a hard-traveled road. There is hope for all beings. The beacons of the light of love bring hope to those who have no hope at all.

To see souls reach and feel their own inner strength and harmony is love in itself. Faith is a starting place. Gentleness will occur. A peaceful approach to achievement will be everlasting. Attainment to one's purpose will unfold with every step and every breath taken. Be a transmitter of love, and hope will occupy your heart.

Angel of
Kindness

Be kind today. Everybody could use a dose of kindness. Express your thoughts with love and let your actions be soft in nature. A simple good deed will refresh the spirit. Send a positive thought to your neighbor or to an animal in need. Find peace at home and let it spread to all with whom you come in contact. Kindness goes farther than hatred. Care about the words you speak and the energy you release. Make sure your expression is based on love, even if you are frustrated. Communicate as a kind soul who wants peace and resolution.

Inspire the hearts and souls of others

to follow your lead. Resist the temptation to behave in a selfish or mean way. Let kindness come naturally.

Walk a path where the foundation allows you to grow and ascend. Allow others, and animals, into your life. Let them share their light to your soul and darkness will soon disappear. Strive for unity as you transcend to your destination.

Spread love through all your travels. Spread it joyfully and unconditionally. You will be provided with protection and warmth. As you grow, so does your love and understanding. As we deepen our comprehension of life, we deepen our love of ourselves. We find compassion in our hearts. Illuminate the world by sharing a spark of love. There is an endless supply. God gives back many times what we give.

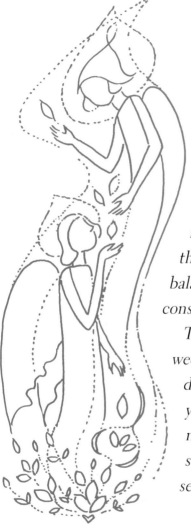

Angel of
Lessons

*T*o experience life means to
experience ups and downs. The key is to
make the downs as few as possible, with
the least amount of disturbance. The more
balanced we become, the more we have
consistent happiness and hope.

The trying times may last an hour, day,
week, month or years. You have the choice to
decide how long. You have your path and
your lessons to learn. Some lessons are
more difficult than other lessons. Some
souls have developed more wisdom and can
see more clearly.

☆

Have faith: The seed has been planted in you. Now let it grow and blossom into that beautiful flower that you are. It takes both rain and sun to provide the nutrients you need.

Feel the presence of God surround and engulf you. With each bloom there is new awareness. Rise above the challenges and blossom. Put your mind toward reaching the summit. As you set your goals and standards, ask God to lead you on your path for your highest good. The earth needs your unique qualities and gifts. Bless others with your soul and your contributions. Appreciate life's lessons. The seed you were born of was a seed from God. Let all your blossoms bloom into their full magnificence.

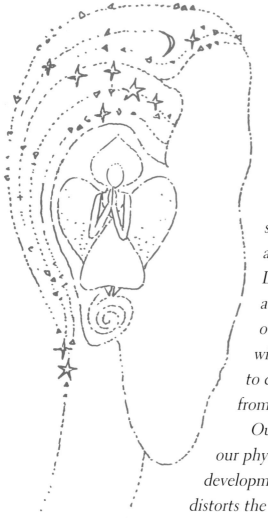

Angel of
Listening

*W*hen you listen to your
soul, you are in balance. This
attainment shows wisdom.
Listening within is the best guide
available. When we listen to
ourselves, we are making contact
with our higher self. It takes insight
to distinguish listening to our wants
from listening to our needs.

Our soul knows before coming into
our physical body what is needed for our
development. It is our mind that clouds and
distorts the process. More and more souls will

be working toward a kinder and softer way. Old ways will collapse and there will be new awakening. Positions that once seemed unreachable will be reached. You can rise and make room for higher learning. Ultimately, blockages will make you stronger and consequences will help you reach wiser insights.

Listen carefully to what you are saying. Pay attention to what you need and to what you are receiving to live a healthy and spiritual life. Our inner voice guides us, but we must listen. When we deny ourselves inner peace and joy, our lives become unmanageable and fearful. Learn to go within and connect with the universal spark. Inside each of us there is a place of hope and strength. It is time to no longer look for someone else to bring us our happiness. We have the potential to tap into our inner well of knowledge anytime that we like. God gives us free choice with our decisions. Use the gift wisely.

Angel of
Living

We walk the road of life with many questions. Our thoughts become our reality. If we believe in our everlasting spirit we will live each day with reverence and awe. The body and soul that does not believe cannot truly live. To live is to love and to love is to have God in our hearts. Living is receiving knowledge. Know that we are provided with an abundance of riches. Tapping into the soul's riches is tapping into our heart. When we unlock the passageway, we find ourselves on a journey, a journey to oneness with God. To breathe as if we were at one with God, is to breathe life. Share your breath of life with others, and let the opulence overflow.

Answers are given when our thoughts are transformed into ideas. When we live with loving and peaceful thoughts, we will create loving and peaceful actions. Remember that God is the highest good. It is our choice to hold that good in our hearts. May you be surrounded with the light of love and the light of direction. The only true light that exists is that of God. Hold on to it and walk in the light. Live your life as a child of God.

Angel of Love

*O*f all the spiritual attributes, love is the greatest. Each being needs the warmth and support of the universal spiritual energy. Every breath of love taken in opens the way to fulfillment and enlightenment. Every breath of love exhaled opens the way for others. Spiritual love then expands into a powerful energy. The more it grows, the stronger it becomes. This is true of the soul. The more wisdom the soul attains, the stronger it becomes.

Every step taken represents a part of the growth cycle. When a step is taken with the love of humankind, the step becomes at one with all. When goodness is at the foundation of every step and every breath taken, there is no challenge that cannot be accepted.

The heart and soul remain intact when centered on the love of one another and in the love of our Infinite Spirit. It is in the darkness of fear that steps are taken toward the destruction of another. To turn all darkness into a flowing stream of the light of love would bring energy too beautiful to describe. May all existing love-light beings share their sparks with all matter. When sparks hit someone or something else, they ignite more sparks. It then becomes a magnificent cycle. For one soul to grow in enlightenment makes another soul look at its own path. This leads more souls to become beacons of the light of love.

Angel of
Luck

We all know people who seem to be very lucky. When the analysis is over, these people usually have the admirable traits of hope, discipline and hard work. The lost and confused often falsely accuse the hard worker of being lucky. They do not see all the actions that go behind the results. When someone does something well, it looks easy and effortless.

Gifts do come to many, but in most cases, these gifts have been earned. They do not have to be understood by all. They just are.

As you progress to a higher spiritual attainment, laziness and apathy go away and are replaced with movement and action. Watch a talented musician play a fine instrument with ease and grace. It is not by luck that he or she plays so well. The musician may have been given the gift of music, but the talent to play so well came from hours of hard work, discipline and dedication. We earn our own luck.

☆

Angels of
Miracles

The power of love creates miracles. You are a miracle. Let your soul share in the miracles of today. Experience the power of love by loving yourself and others. On your path you will touch the lives of others, giving others love, hope and trust. All miracles start with love and build with hope.

When it is for your highest good, a miracle will occur. Believe and be ready. Accept the energy of love and the light of good. Encourage all to be open to the love of God. Find the miracles in your life. They are all around you.

Angels of
Mission

To find your mission is to find enlightenment. Many know their missions, as they know their names, others struggle and never know their missions. When the mind is clear and the body is in balance, clarity comes. An inner voice is heard.

Many along the path get sidetracked and through their own free will ignore their true calling. Do not settle for anything less than what you want. Harmony is yours if you want it. Be willing to let go and give up what is not working so you can let new opportunities present themselves.

Strength comes from being open-minded. Broaden your horizons and see that there are no limits, except the ones you make.

Discover your gifts and carry the strength of the universe within you. When you follow God's will for you, you will find the highest achievement of peace and serenity you have ever experienced. New and exciting vistas will open for you. Your gifts will expand to added dimensions. You will experience a deeper standard of excitement. This will be your passion.

Appreciate who you are and face life with an energy of love. The more you radiate with a desire for life, the more life will treat you with the love you want. Unlock the potential you have inside and take the risks to find who you are.

Serenity comes when we stay on course with our mission. When others see the serenity we have by being steadfast to our mission, we bring hope to them. May you take hold of your mission. God is with you all the way.

☆

Angel of
Opportunity

We are given many opportunities to expand our consciousness. Often we do not seize them. You have to be ready. You have to be willing to step in a new direction. Serenity is found when fear is gone. Serenity comes when you take the opportunity to grow. The mind that thinks it knows all, knows little.

Walk in the light of sunshine. You can be the sunshine that spreads light wherever you go. You can make a difference in your own life and in the lives of others. Fatigue is replaced with strength. Anger is replaced with calm. Hate is replaced with love. Selfishness is replaced with generosity. All bad is replaced with all good.

Good thinking changes the way we look at every situation, even the ones that are difficult. We learn a new way of handling our behavior. Results will only inspire the importance of the consciousness of our thoughts. All thoughts go somewhere. Always keep that in mind and remember you are responsible for your life.

Acceptance starts with love, love for being who you are. Each day is an opportunity to love and grow, and be at one with all.

Angel of
Peace

We are not here to be at war with
one another. While you may not agree with
others, there is no need to have hatred in your
heart. The more we find the doorway to the
Divine the more open-minded and tolerant we are
of others. Love and harmony equal peace. Peace starts
with you. Do you have peace within? The first place to
make peace is within your soul. Then you will carry peace
wherever you go. Peace is the result of trusting in our
Creator. When the mind and body are calm, vibrations of
love and harmony touch the hearts of others. Go spread
your peace and watch your life change.

We were born to love one another. To love another we must love ourselves. In order to grow we have to come back to love. You don't grow by hating yourself, your neighbor, or the world.

Love starts within and grows outward. When we go against our natural rhythm of love, we are out of balance. The universe is constantly showing us how to get back to love. Listen and see your voyage with clarity. Find the love in your heart and share it.

Trust that you will see love as the foundation of all. It is the breath of life. As we breathe with life, we act with love. Believe in your heart and soul that we are all made in the likeness of God. Make peace with all with whom you come in contact. Forgive the wrongs of others as you try to better your own thoughts and actions. Go spread love to yourself and others. The rewards are measureless.

Angel of
Potential

Gracefully bloom into the rich creation that you are. Touch the inner strength that lies inside, around and behind you: it is your potential. We have a source we can go to, talk to and pray to when we need help. God is available at all times for our every need. We might use other resources for guidance and assistance, but God is the force behind all healing.

We are often blinded by the magnitude of our problems. Our lives become filled with despair. We lose track of our potential. When the mind, body and soul work together, love and wisdom surfaces,

and the root of all problems are dealt
with to achieve victory.

We face our choices somewhere in
time. There is always a way for help and
development. The meaning of our
existence is to discover the spiritual being
we can be, and become at one with God.
We learn through our lessons.

We have potential that lays dormant. We
have the potential to grow to greater heights at all
times. Do not judge yourself by someone else's
potential. Utilize your own. Create the path that
will let you be your highest self.

Angel of
Practice

As you go through the day, be conscious of your every thought and every word spoken. Replace any negative thoughts or words with positive and supportive ones. If you cannot come up with any then let them go. Release the negative energy both in mind and action. You will find your day to be more uplifting and inviting. God will be seen, heard, and felt. As you practice this exercise, it becomes a way of living. Treasures will be apparent when the cleansing is done.

Practice the exercise of peace. Close your eyes and rest your mind. Picture yourself surrounded by a calming energy. Let the energy soak into your pores, filling your body with love and healing. As it goes throughout your body, experience the tingling sensations. Be ready to heal any negative emotion or sickness. The more you love and take care of yourself, the more you can enjoy the abundance of living life to its fullest.

Practice the exercise of laughter. Laugh today. Wear a smile and let it start from the inside out. Take time off from being so serious. Realize that we must enjoy the moment. Projecting too far into the future or concentrating too much on our troubles prevents the child in us from coming out. We all need more love, smiles, flowers and laughter in our lives. Start with yourself. You'll find it is contagious.

Angel of
Praise

*Y*ou are a gift, beautiful from the inside out. You are
here for a special reason. Know you are loved and you
love. Realize you are okay just the way you are, right
now. Open to the light of God and shine as a star, a
star of love. Be ready to experience praise in your life.
When you express yourself as child of God, good will
result. You can help make a difference in other lives.
Know this and seek the road where all creations are
equal. You are wonderful and needed today and every
day. Accept praise with grace.

We look in the mirror and for years we are not sure
whom we see. We question the reflection. As we work

☆

☆

through our lessons and work our way to finding explanations, we learn we are at one with God. We can have an abundance of riches, inside and out, if we allow our highest good to come into our lives.

The first step for any growth, anywhere and anytime, is belief in yourself. When you love yourself you are loving God's creation. We were meant to be at one with God. We were meant to share in love and happiness. Open your heart and let the universal energy of love pour in.

☆

Angel of
Prosperity

*T*here are no limits except those you create. You can have an
abundance or riches when you live by the rule of abundance and not of
limitation. You deserve to be blessed with prosperity. True prosperity
comes when you are doing what your heart truly desires. When you are
using all your talents and gifts with God as the foundation, prosperity
will come.

Money is not the source of prosperity. It is only a tool. Open yourselves to the new energy and vibration that exists. Simply listen to the voice inside. Be surrounded with love and goodness. Let all that does not bring you happiness be removed. Picture yourself receiving the gifts of abundance. You have the right to let the wind of spirituality push you to triumphs of abundance. Don't be afraid to sail off on the course that is right for you. A course that brings fulfillment to the heart will bring prosperity to the soul.

Angel of
Purpose

*C*hanges in your plan can be taken more gracefully when you are aware of your soul's plan. Develop new ways to look at the total picture to determine your soul's purpose. Your maturity grows and your actions reflect the handling of change. Steps taken in acceptance and peace far outweigh steps taken in resentment and fear. Those who realize the purpose of their soul's plan achieve higher understanding. The highly developed soul uses every situation as a learning experience and accepts it as part of the soul's cycle.

Be careful not to judge others. You do not have access to all their data or their purpose. You can serve only as a helper and must attend to your own purpose.

The mature soul prays for those in need of guidance and direction, and does not judge or gossip.

During periods of the soul's cycle, the soul is faced with different situations in which we may fulfill our earthly wants but lose sight of the purpose our soul's plan. These decisions and choices can affect our ongoing growth. Many times we have to retrace our steps. Wisdom takes time and is earned. The beauty of all souls is the reaching of higher wisdom where peace lies. To feel this depth of happiness and true harmony within the soul makes one want to continue on this journey. Once this is experienced, the soul desires more of this harmony. Only by keeping the purpose of our soul's plans in all our thoughts and actions can we stay on the holy path.

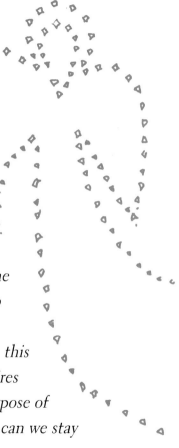

Angel of
Sea

The mystical magic of the sea. The sea is continually delivering messages to help any voyage be a successful one. Listen carefully as the elements of the land meet the elements of the sea. When the heart and mind become one, we sail a blissful journey. As a vessel sets sail, the rules of the sea become apparent. Rules of the sea, the great truths, have existed from the beginning of time. It is up to each vessel to practice the teachings and carry the messages to help other vessels on their voyages.

Water your soul with the sea of spirituality. Cross each passage with hope. Let courage be your outlook. The sea will forever flow as your soul swims in this world of oneness.

To understand the great mysteries of life, one must live the great mysteries of life. Self-discovery comes through experiences. Continuous wars are no solution. The power of authority is not force. The time has come for the world to wake up. Wake up to the power inside every soul. Let that power be one of love for one another.

Do not turn your back on others. No, turn your ear to them. Listen with compassion. Find compassion in your heart. Live with love. Give of yourself. It is time to bring the sea to meet the land and bring spirituality home. Your true home is with God. Search no longer.

Angel of
Self-Love

*T*aking notices of our strengths helps build
our self-love. Nurturing allows healing to take
place on a spiritual level. We were not always
conditioned to love ourselves. The time has come
where all living creatures need to love
themselves as well as each other. Every soul has
something to love. Every soul needs to be loved.
In times of difficulty, chaotic energy can create a
downward cycle. We find it hard to love ourselves.
Souls must unite and have love and understanding
for each other, and let go of hate and resentment.
The weaknesses we share need to be addressed. Let go

of the bad and replace it with good. Let go of chaos and replace it with order. We need to improve our self-love.

Every soul is different. Every soul has its own lessons. Every soul has a path. We can teach our beliefs, but wisdom is earned. First, accept your lessons and it will be easier to accept others. Do not measure all by what you see. Before trying to work on another, try working on yourself. The beauty of living comes from the beauty of self-love.

Self-love comes when we realize the importance of our every thought and action. While lessons are happening continually, the way we choose to handle them makes all the difference. Ask for help and turn things over. Pour out energy of goodness and goodness will come to you. Your efforts will be rewarded with infinite self-love.

Angel of *Soul*

In the journey of life you begin to question your actions and your purpose for existence at different times. This is a good sign. When you connect with the celestial heavens and learn to flow with the energy, great accomplishments are made. Success comes from within and cannot be measure by outward materialistic goods. This does not mean the successful spiritual person cannot share in nice and material things. All thoughts and intentions should be balanced.

The universe brings us answers on a continual basis. It is the human who refuses to pay attention. The soul stands back until an understanding comes through. Finding and sharing the truth ultimately soothes the struggling and confused soul.

Discover the world within, and then you will let the world discover you. Every soul has a journey to take. A journey that will be decided by you. To realize we make our own happiness or unhappiness is to realize the truth. When peace and happiness find a home within your soul, you will instinctively know the strength of God, therefore, know the strength of your own wisdom.

Every road taken, rocky or smooth, has wisdom to be learned. When your soul is rich in wisdom, fear and the choices which are not of God's will are eliminated. Each phase of life will call on different wisdom to lead the way. The first step is the step for guidance. May all walk toward the path where the steps are taken though the wisdom and guidance of our Creator. ☆

Angel of Sounds

Listen to the silence. Hear the sounds of peace. Clear
the mind and become a channel for higher energies.
Reach for the stillness that brings contact with God. By
quieting the mind, harmonious energy flows through
us. Accept the messages of wisdom that are brought
forth. Embrace the warm energy. You are just where you
need to be. It is by Divine order. Raise your consciousness
to higher thinking. Watch the fears fall away. Watch your
perspective change. Learn what is important. Speak carefully
of others. Know your thoughts produce energy somewhere.
Let it be the energy of love. The world is in need of silence.
Silence and love carry the message.

☆

The world is full of sounds: some good, some not so good, but many are unimportant. Tune in to only what you need to hear. Train your ears to receive only the good sounds. But not all sounds come from outside oneself, just as many come from within. Be open to your inner voice and the voice of God. Chimes of peace come from wanting the best for you and for others. Keep your body, mind and soul in tune and radiate with vibrations of peace. Listen to the sea and what do you hear? Words of hope, waves of strength. Draw upon the unseen force for protection. Leave behind the storms and drift into the current of love, hope and trust. Take the good sounds that you hear and pass them along to those in need. Sounds of love leave vibrations of hope.

Angel of
Speaking

The tongue can be sharp and out of control. Harsh words leave scars and trigger angry emotions, It is important to voice your feelings in a healthy way. Some circumstances seem unfair and our reactions may be strong.

Go within and find yourself. Then speak with self-love and love for your neighbor. When we speak peacefully, without hate and fear, others are more prone to listen. Words have great power and should be taken seriously. Expressing your soul is important. Let the expression be one of truth. The truth needs to be heard. The word needs to be spoken with love from the heart and not with anger from the voice.

Angel of Success

*T*ake time to relax and go within. Quieting the mind allows new energy to come. Enjoy what you do. Make your work a hobby. Add excitement to your life by living your life with passion. Use all your abilities. Let God be your starting place and then move outward. You do not have to be understood by all. As a spiritual child you never walk alone. God is within you and outside you. When you know this, all things are possible. Let go of the fears that inhibit your creativity. Invest by treating yourself with nurturing thoughts of love and respect.

Use your passion to stretch your mind by asking questions. Figure out how to leave something better than how you found it. Decide what you want and go after it. Do not be limited by material goods. Use your mind to overcome obstacles. Treat each obstacle as an opportunity to grow and develop the creative spirit.

Success comes in many different ways, but not always on the first try. Usually, when we don't achieve success on the first try, we learn valuable lessons that enable us to achieve a success greater than we had planned. You must channel your energy in the direction you want to go. Believe in yourself, and others will follow. Use your passion to tap into the resources that are stored in your soul.

Appreciate what you have and love what you don't have. Do not compare yourself to others. Trust in your own path and in your own creativity. Use your gifts and you will be given more. When you use your talents wisely, the soul is in harmony. All gifts are meant to be shared. Be good to yourself and you will be good to others. Your passion will give you the strength.

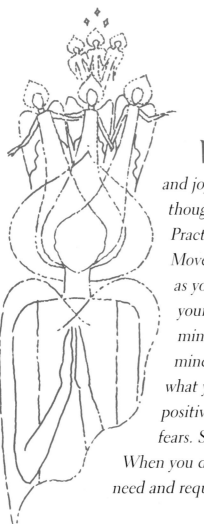

Angel of
Thoughts

*W*elcome thoughts that bring warmth and joy into your soul. Learn to let go of thoughts that are troubling and disturbing. Practice concentrating on love and peace. Move your vibrations to higher realizations as you open the passageway to truth. Let your action reflect the thoughts you hold in mind. Know that the thoughts held in mind, produce after their kind. You create what you want. Take the steps to bring positive influences into your life. Release fears. Security comes in trusting in God. When you direct your thoughts to God, your every need and request is heard.

Thoughts are energy and they must go somewhere. The more the universe can share in positive loving energy, the closer we come to individual and worldwide peace. You and your thoughts make a difference. Use them wisely. Discover the power within yourself to change your life. By changing your attitude you set the energy in a different motion. When the attitude is changed for the better, better gifts come. Keep the mind healthy, and the body and soul will be healthy. Let new thoughts be a reflection of your personal growth.

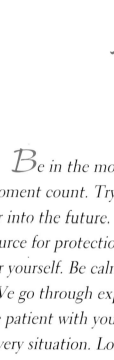

Angel of Time

Be in the moment. Live in the present. Make every moment count. Try to release the past and not project too far into the future. Relinquish control and let God be your source for protection and direction. Pray for others and pray for yourself. Be calm even in the midst of turbulent times. We go through experiences to become stronger and wiser. Be patient with yourself and others. Look for the best in every situation. Look for the best in everyone you meet. With love and trust at the foundation of your heart, you will become more accepting of the present moment. Walk with your eyes forward. Greet time with opportunities. We came from God and must be with God. Do not wait to be with God some other time. Know you are with God at all times.

Time is a block to many. If you are living life in fast motion, you are not allowing for tenderness and love. It is good to be productive, but is also good to slow down long enough to express love and kindness along the way.

More and more people will be seeking a lifestyle where time will be used to provide for inner needs as well as outer needs. They will want work for a life that is more rewarding and joyful. Time with family and nature will be important. Making this happen takes discipline, especially if this is new to you. Live in the present.

☆

Angel of
Trust

When bonds of trust are broken, the damage goes further than the eye can see. Honesty builds friendship, lies build distance. Fear and shame are the roots of dishonesty.

When you truly love yourself, the truth will be shown. Until self-worth is established, the truth might be too painful to face. When you lie to cover up something it might work for that moment, but in *reality it eventually comes out. The results are more damaging than if you were honest from the beginning.*

To face up to something is difficult because you must own the truth. You who live your life on principles of dishonesty are weak and frightened. If you have been lied to by someone you trusted, ask why you were attracted to that person. It is painful to lose trust in a loved one or friend.

Be honest and trustworthy, and know that those traits will carry you in times of adversity and suffering.

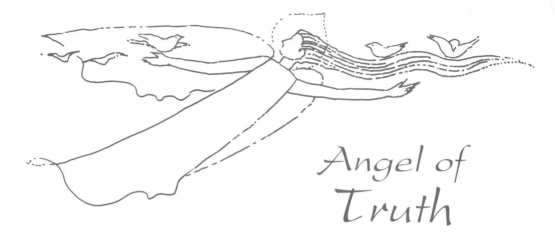

Angel of Truth

*T*he wise accepts the truth and speaks the truth, though it might be hard to face. The truth wins and comes to light. We cannot run from the truth. When you learn to be honest and true, life can be faced with courage, strength and goodness. Then loving results are achieved. If you turn to lies and deceptions, your life becomes self-destructive.

Speak the truth and the truth shall be heard. Truth will always conquer. The truth cannot be silent for too long. The higher self can always turn to the universe for the truth. God will speak. It is up to us to listen.

Create an environment with only the truth and the highest good, and you will have it. Then you will be surrounded with purer energy and higher vibrations. The vibrations are in synchronization with your natural harmony. When obstacles present themselves, hold strong and the truth will let you rise above them.

Angel of
Understanding

*U*se your mind, body and spirit to find
the purpose of your life. Once you have inner
peace and clarity, your purpose becomes a
reality of life. Life is no longer a mystery.
There are still challenges, but they can be
looked at in a different way and with a clearer
perspective. Understand and know that
everything we do is for the sole purpose of
becoming one with God. To express opposite
vibrations is going against God's will.

The mysteries of life do not have to be
mysteries. Mysteries are mysteries because we do

not understand them. Understanding comes as the soul searches and achieves wisdom.

A spark of information or an affirmation often is all it takes to lead one to their spiritual path and purpose. With faith and dedication to one's faith, comes greater understanding of the truth of life. While it is painful and frustrating to see some souls take longer or struggle harder to resolve their own mysteries, it is an individual process that they must go through. We can give our love and support, and share our growth and knowledge, but they must seek their answer.

Angel of
Unfoldment

T he mind is extremely fascinating. It longs to
know answers, yet it does not always know the direction to
take to find them. Your path is a way for the soul to develop
wisdom and become a soul for higher learning. All souls
have a place for advancement. Do not be discouraged no
matter where you are. By honoring your soul, your
spiritual path will unfold with Divine timing. Be patient.
The beauty of life is clear when all souls work together
to create a welcoming place where everyone is accepted. A

☆

highly developed spiritual soul can show others the way – the way where a new start can transform into a beautiful journey. A smile or hug makes the surrounding more peaceful. Humor is essential for growth. It is important not to take any situation too seriously. Souls are never alone, even in the deepest valleys of loneliness. There are others waiting to help souls unfold when the help is wanted.

When we get weary and our shoulders get heavy, we can summon the celestial guardians to help carry our burdens. God works in mysterious ways. Because many souls are turned off or confused about the word of God, they don't ask for help. The earth needs to be restored with spiritual energy that allows people to be enriched by universal energy. With time, a troubled soul will seek out its own relationship with God and embrace its spiritual journey. The starting point begins with inner awareness. Watching the way the path unfolds is an experience of beauty and strength.

Angel of
Wisdom

Wisdom comes through every waking experience. The key is to stand back and take a look at what works and feels loving and right for all concerned. Our souls are much less troubled when we treat them properly. When we go against God's will, it only creates turmoil and fear.

Our soul develops and gathers wisdom. It recognizes and stays away from negative influences and wrongdoing. The soul can constantly reach new vibrations and exalted levels of learning. Some souls are here to help other souls find their paths, lending assistance in that direction. It brings much peace and comfort to know your help and touch might be all it takes to help others on their journey. It is important not to judge others. We are not the authority. All these words sound so simple, but for many, they are too far away to reach.

There are all kinds of souls with different missions and different levels of wisdom. As your soul develops, the more at peace it becomes while growing closer in the oneness with God. A change in thought will change action. May all strive for this goal.

Beauty and peace lie in an unseen force – a force so powerful that it is indescribable. Faith is needed in all lives. With the faith of God, miracles occur. It is wonderful for those who have God in their hearts to share their wisdom with others, in hopes that they, too, can reach fulfillment in their lives.

☆

Other books and journals
by Samara Anjelae

100 Ways to Attract Angels
My Guardian Angel
My Fairy Godmother
My Magical Mermaid
Wonder Windows Gift Box
Fairy Journal: Thoughts & Dreams
Gnome Journal: Notes & Musings

www.belletressbooks.com

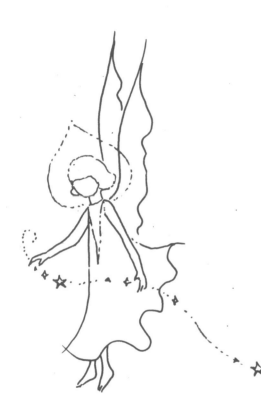